Match the Elephant Parts

Add ears, eyes, trunk, legs, and tail stickers to complete the elephant's body.

T0019396

Match the Zebra Parts

Add ear, eye, nose, legs, and tail stickers to complete the zebra's body.

Make a Pattern on the Giraffe

Add stickers to the giraffe to create its pattern.

example

Sticker

Good job!

3

In the Sea

Put stickers wherever you'd like to create an underwater scene.

example

In the Sky

Put stickers wherever you'd like to create a scene in the sky.

On a Safari

What animals do you see on a safari? Put each animal sticker on its matching shadow.

On a Farm

What animals do you see on a farm? Put each animal sticker on its matching shadow. Then, give each animal a sticker of what they would like.

Sticker

Good job!

sticker

sticker

sticker

sticker

sticker

sticker

sticker

Guess the Animal

Guess the animal from its body part. When you identify the animal, put a sticker on its shadow.

Vehicle Match

Each picture shows the front of a vehicle. Put a sticker next to the vehicle that shows it from the side.

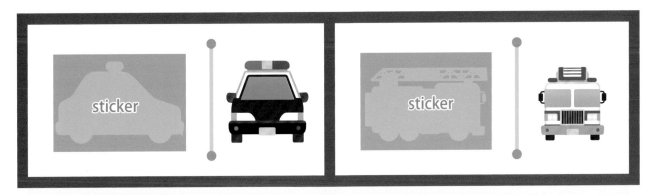

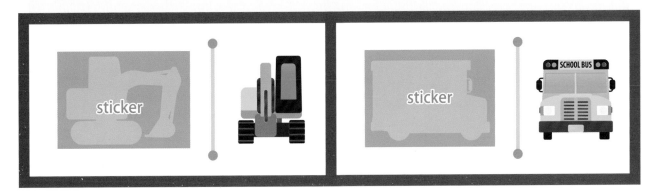

These Things Go Together

Find the stickers that go together and put them in each group (for example: vehicles, animals, fruit).

vehicles

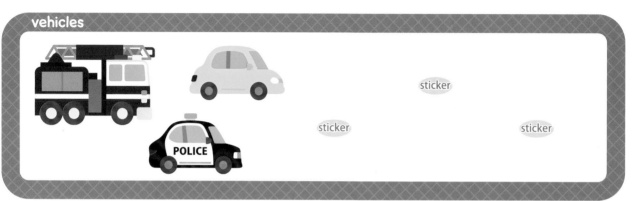

sticker

sticker

sticker

animals

sticker

sticker

sticker

fruit

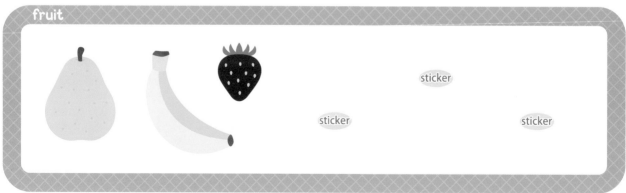

sticker

sticker

sticker

Complete the Picture

Put the matching sticker next to each object to complete the picture.

Sticker

Good job!

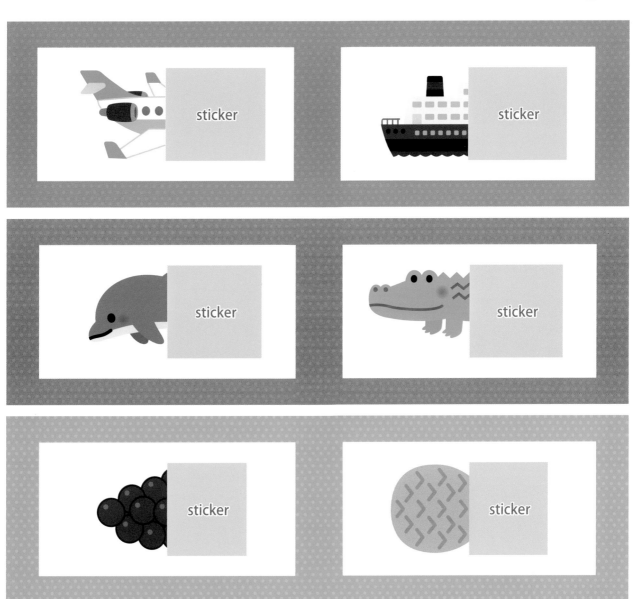

11

Finish the Picture

Add stickers to finish each picture so that it matches the example.

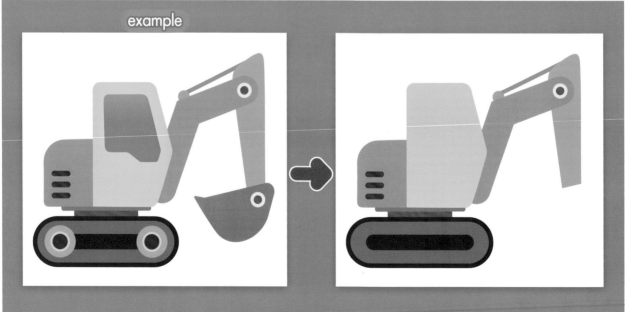

12

Picture Scramble

Do you know the animal in the scrambled picture? Name the animal, then add stickers to complete the picture.

Sticker

Good job!

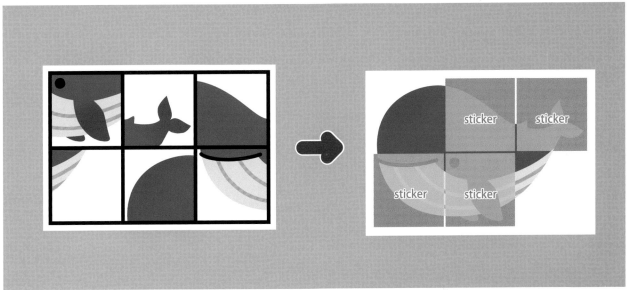

Animal Search

Find the animals hidden in the picture. Then, put the matching sticker in the box.

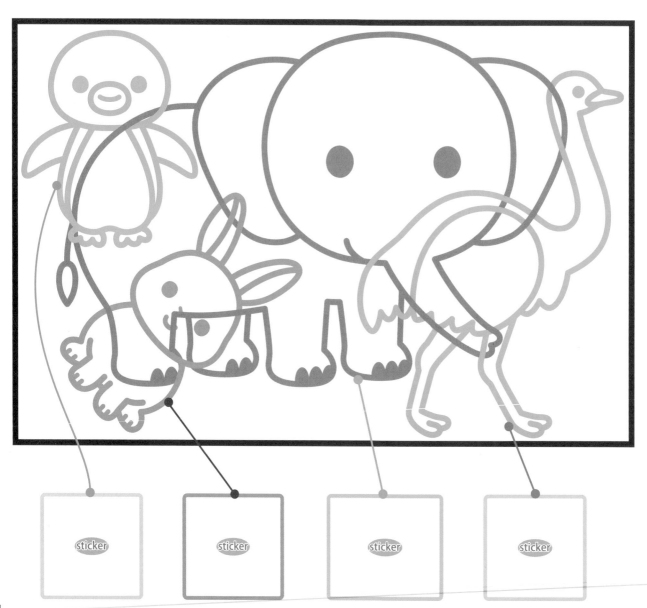

sticker   sticker   sticker   sticker

Vegetable Search

Find the vegetables hidden in the picture. Then, put the matching sticker in the box.

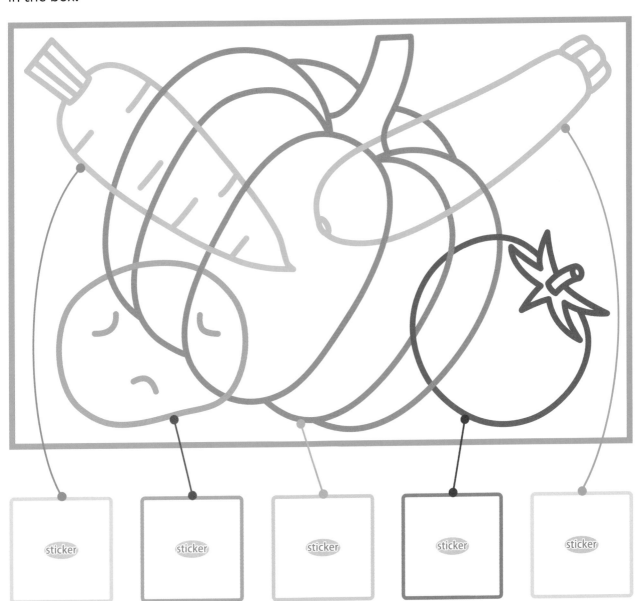

Busy Garden

Put a bee sticker on each flower.

Hungry Hamsters

Give each hamster a seed sticker.

Make a Stylish Ghost

Put a bow tie sticker on each ghost.

example

Sticker

Good job!

Make a Funny Monster

Put eyes, nose, mouth, and arms stickers on each monster.

example

Sticker

Good job!

19

Pattern Puzzle

Follow the pattern in the example to create the same pattern in the boxes on the right.

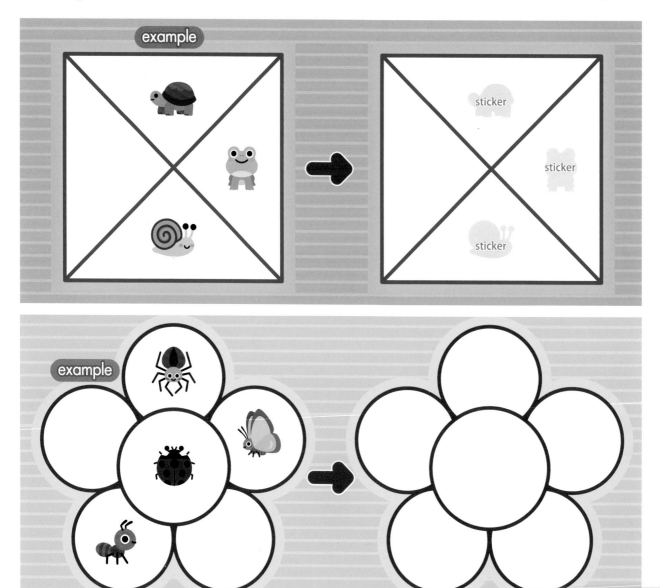

Pattern Puzzle

Follow the pattern in the example to create the same pattern in the boxes on the right.

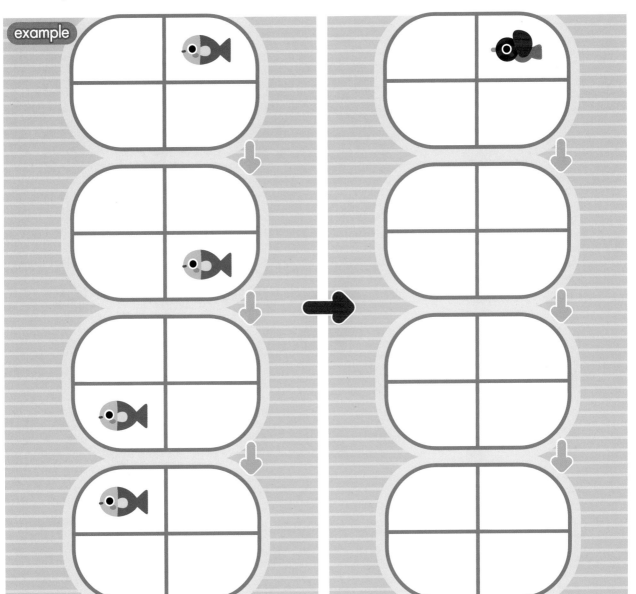

What Is Missing?

Add fruit stickers to the bottom plate so it matches the top plate.

example

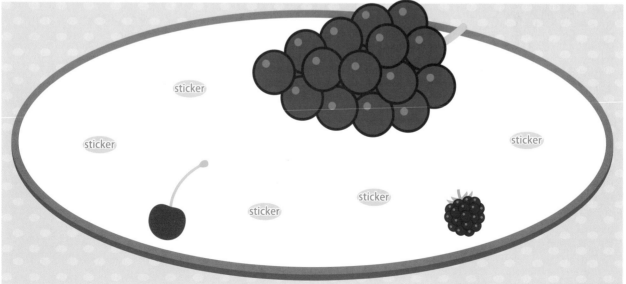

Match the Shadows

The shadows on the left are made up of three fruits. Find the missing fruit stickers and add them to each group.

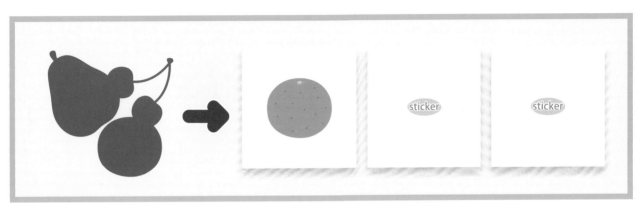

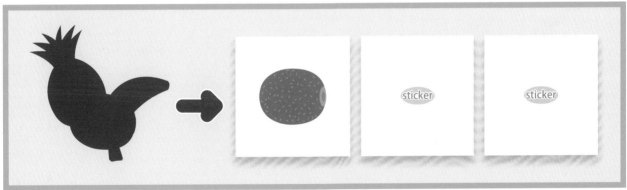

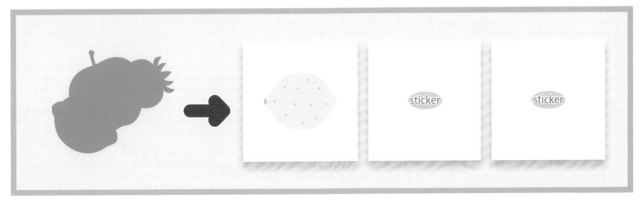

Length and Height

Put each snake sticker in the blank space that matches its size.
Then, do the same for the giraffe stickers.

Good job!

Weight and Size

Match the animal stickers to their shadows, then put extra stickers anywhere you'd like. Which animal is heavier? Which animal is bigger?

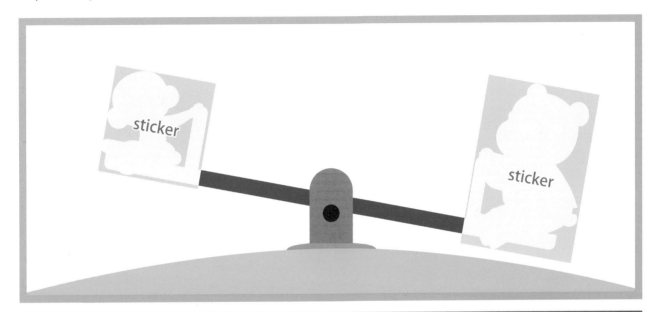

25

Things That Start with A

Say the name of each thing in the letter A. Then, put the matching sticker on sticker .

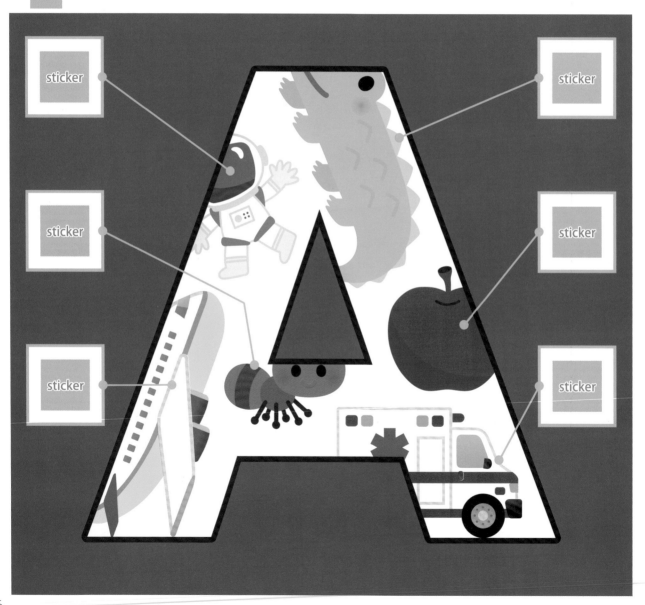

Things That Start with B

Say the name of each thing in the letter B. Then, put the matching sticker on sticker .

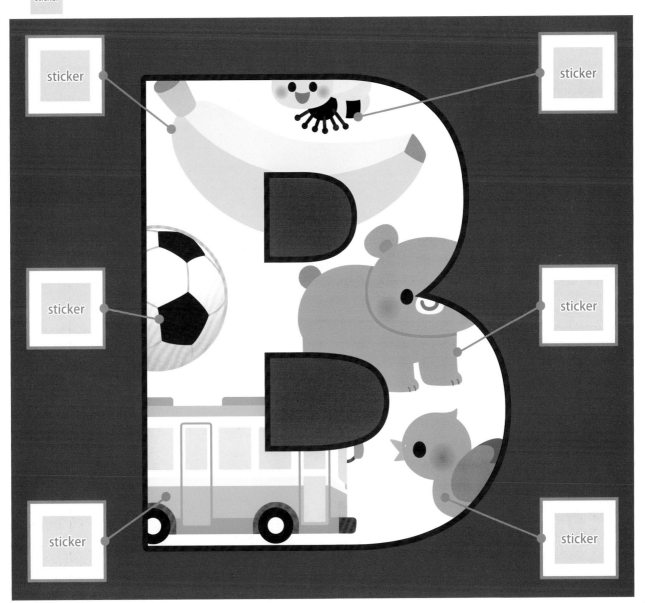

ABC Maze

Follow the path in the order of the alphabet. As you go, put the letter stickers on the path. Then, put stickers on the matching  sticker.

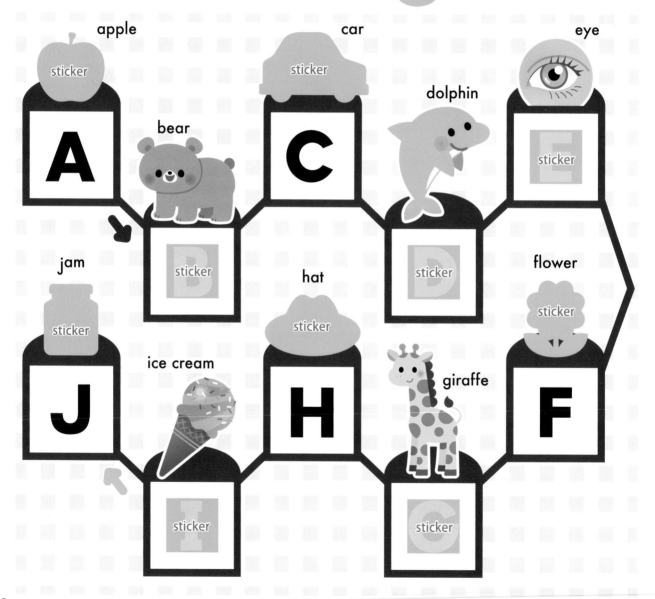

apple

car

eye

dolphin

bear

A

C

E
sticker

jam

B
sticker

hat

D
sticker

flower

J

ice cream

H

giraffe

F

I
sticker

G
sticker

Numbers and Quantity

Add stickers on 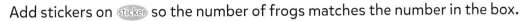 sticker so the number of frogs matches the number in the box.

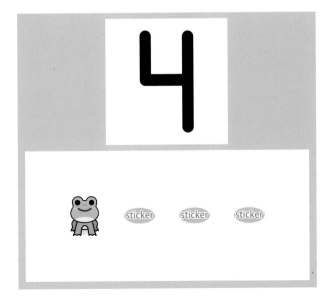

Numbers and Quantity

Add stickers on  so the number of stars matches the number in the box.

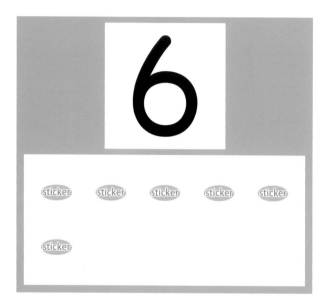

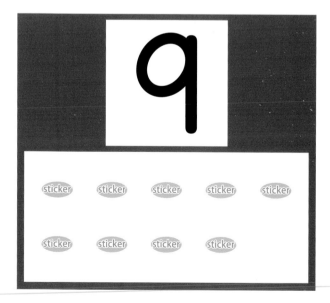

Numbers and Quantity

Add stickers on sticker so the number of flowers matches the number in the box.

Sticker

Good job!

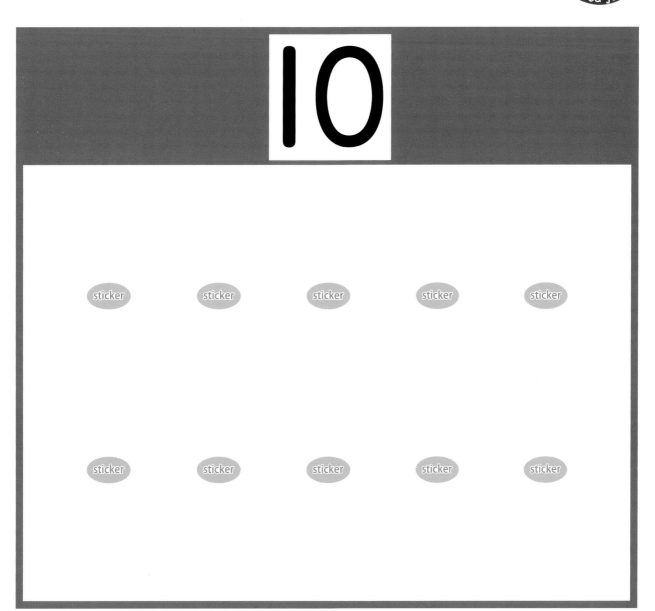

Count the Animals

Count the elephant and hippos in the picture and add the matching number stickers on  sticker . Then, look at the number next to the lion. Add that many lion stickers to the picture.

Count the Insects

Count the butterflies and ladybugs in the picture and add the matching number stickers on sticker . Then, look at the number next to the ant. Add that many ant stickers to the picture.

Sticker

Good job!

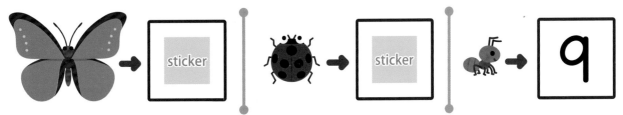

Number Match

Add stickers so there are four goldfish in each fishbowl.

Sticker
Good job!

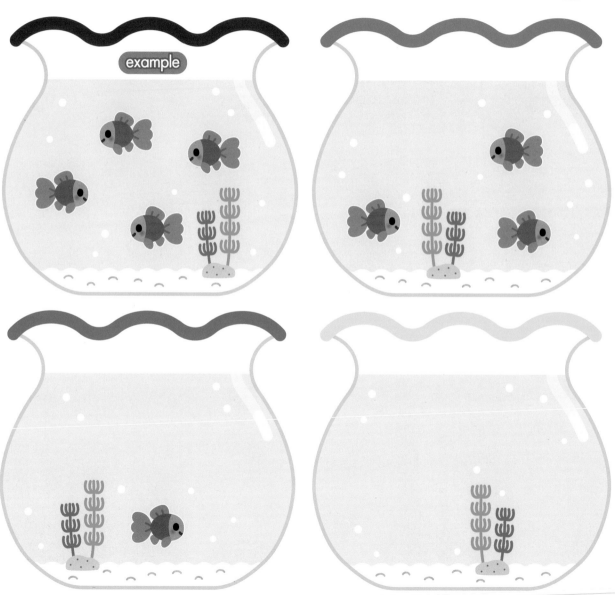

example

Squirrel's Favorite Food

Follow the path from ➡ to ➡. Always go in the direction of the larger number of treats. As you pass through each group, put a squirrel sticker on the space with the larger number. Then, put flower stickers wherever you'd like.

Number Maze

Follow the path from ➡ to ➡ in order of smallest to largest. As you go, put number stickers on the path. When finished, count the number of rabbits.

Good job!

Snack Time

Feed each animal an apple, a banana, and a watermelon sticker.

Sticker
Good job!

Shapes in the Sea

Put the matching sticker on each shape to create sea creatures.

Shapes on the Farm

Put the matching sticker on each shape to create farm animals.

39

Fruit Maze

Follow the path from ➡ to ➡ while putting fruit stickers on their matching shadows.

Good job!

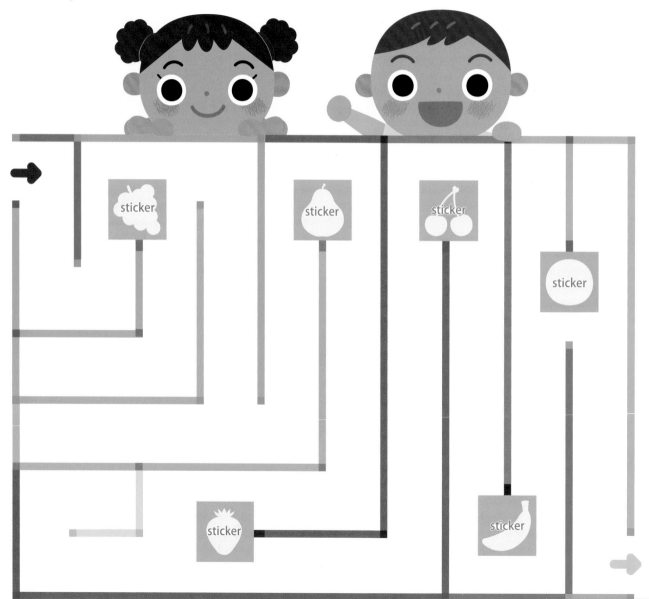

Choo Choo Train

Follow the path from to ➡ while putting stickers on the missing parts of the railroad track. Then, put animal stickers wherever you'd like.

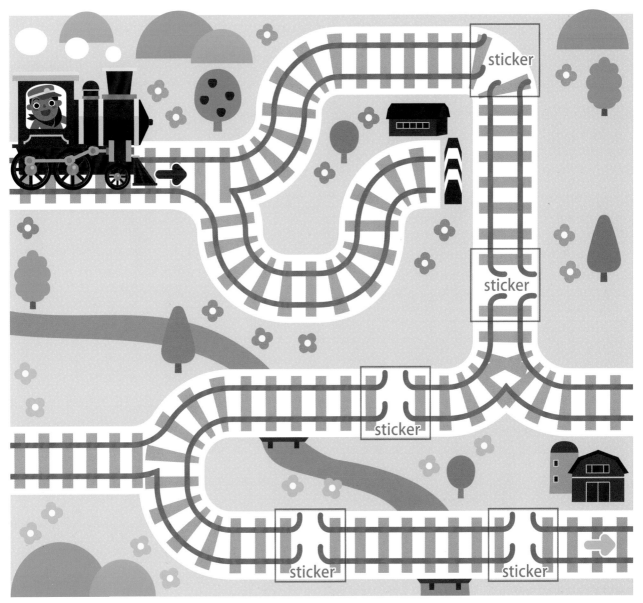

41

Connect the Islands

Connect the islands with bridge stickers so the big mouse can get to the little mouse.

Haunted Maze

Follow the path from ➡ to ➡ while putting ladder stickers on the missing parts.

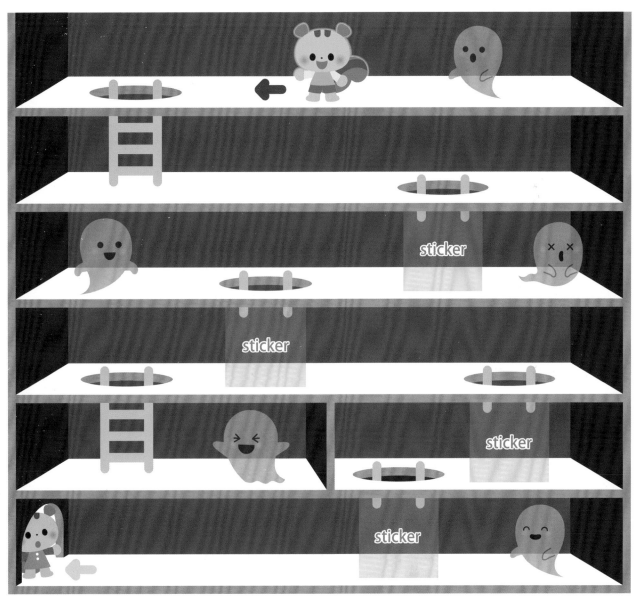

43

In the Garden

Put each insect sticker on its matching shadow.

In the Meadow

Put each animal sticker on its matching shadow. Then, put the extra stickers wherever you'd like.

Sticker

Good job!

45

A Colorful Tree

Put leaf stickers on the tree. Then, add extra stickers to the scene.

example

Sticker
Good job!

A Happy Hedgehog

Decorate the hedgehog's back with colorful △ stickers.

example

Sticker

Good job!

47

Train Puzzle

Put stickers on the train so they match the shapes and colors.

Page 1

Page 2

Page 3

Page 4

Page 6

Page 5

Page 7

Page 8

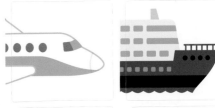

Page 9
Page 10
Page 12
Page 11

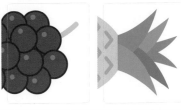

Page 13
Page 14
Page 16

Page 15

Page 17

Page 19

Page 20

Stickers

Page 18

Page 22

Page 21

Page 23

Page 25

Page 24

Page 26

 astronaut
 ant
 airplane
 alligator
 apple
 ambulance

 banana
 ball
 bus
 bee
 bear
 bird

Page 27

B D E G I

Page 28

Page 36

Pages 29–30

Page 31

Page 35

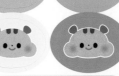

2

3

5

7

q

Page 32

1
2

6
8

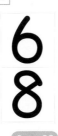

Page 33

Page 37

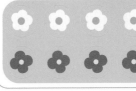

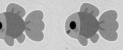

Page 34

Page 38

Page 39

Page 40

Page 41

Page 42

Page 43

Page 44

Page 45

Page 46

Page 48

Page 47